MW00587115

Dressing up

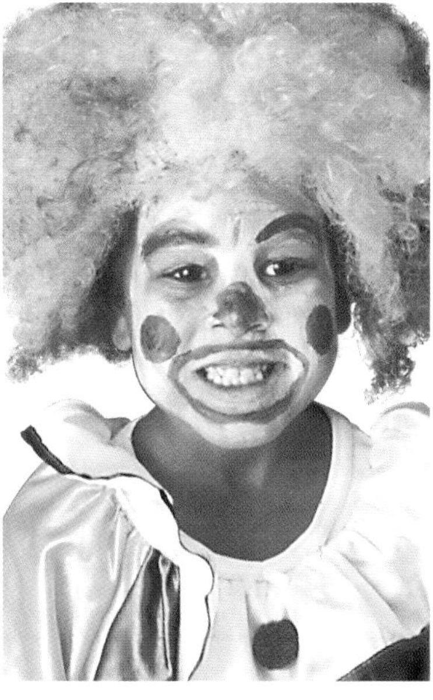

I am a rabbit.

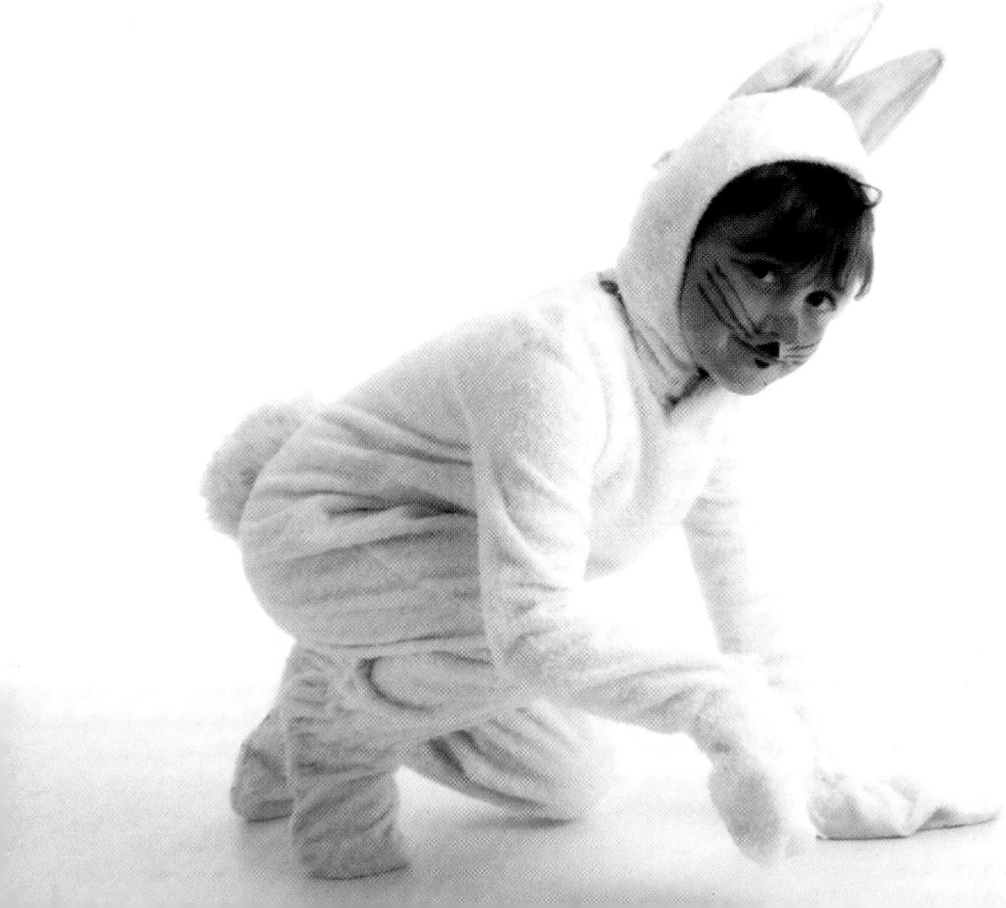

I am a cat.

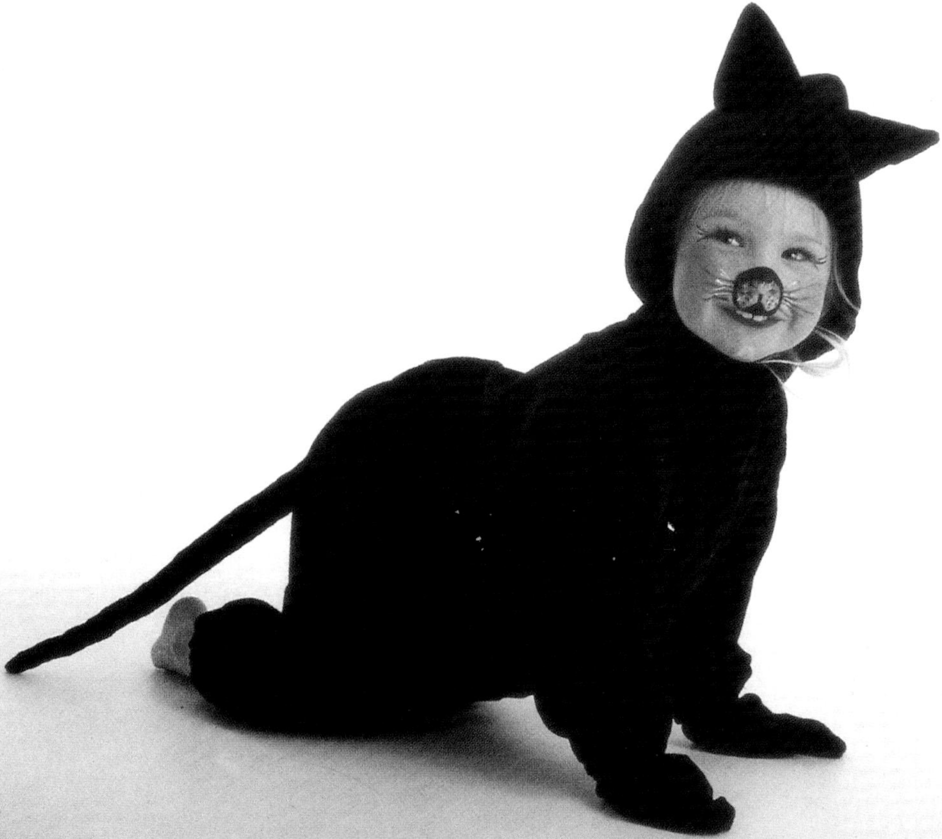

I am a cowboy.

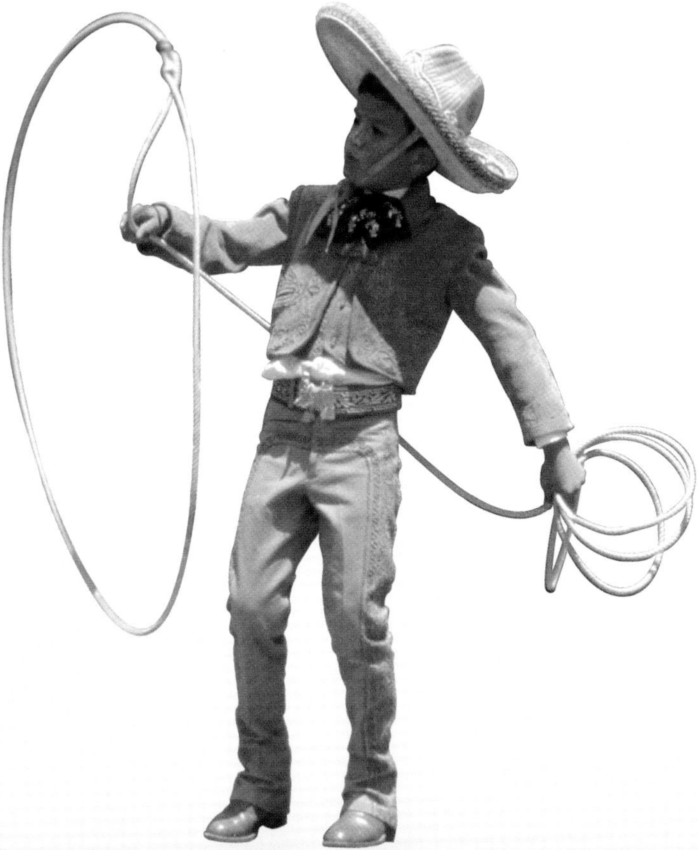

I am a clown.

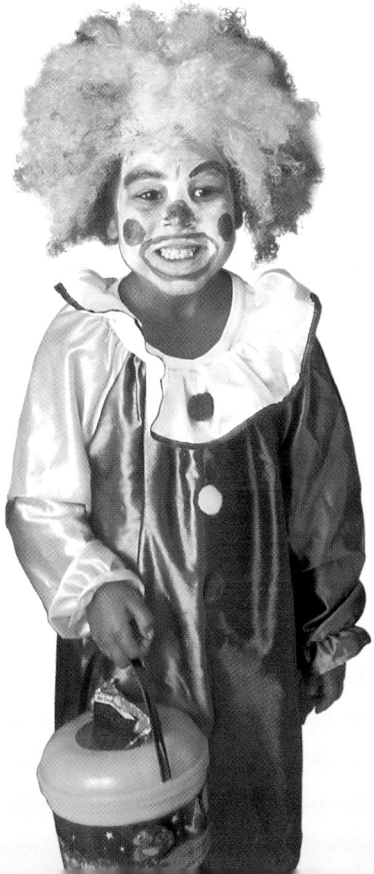

I am a pirate.

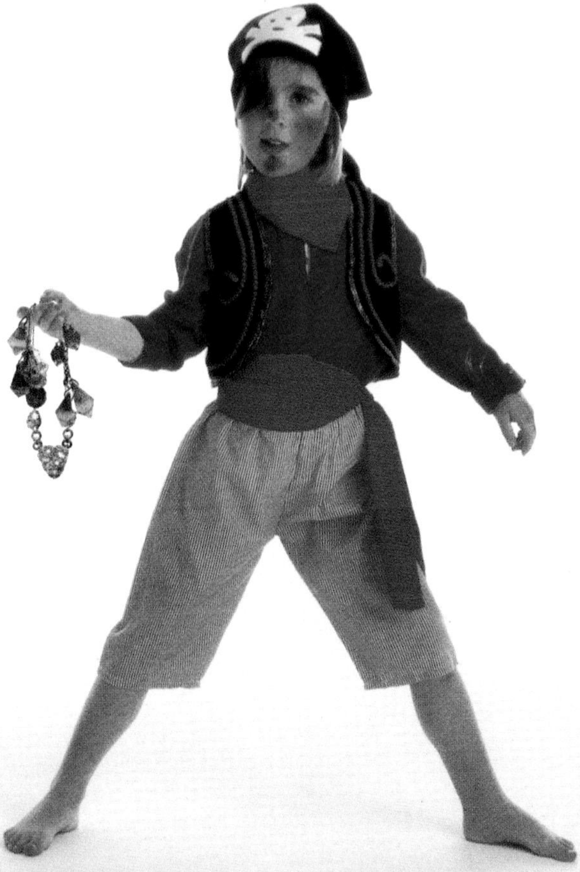

I am a butterfly.

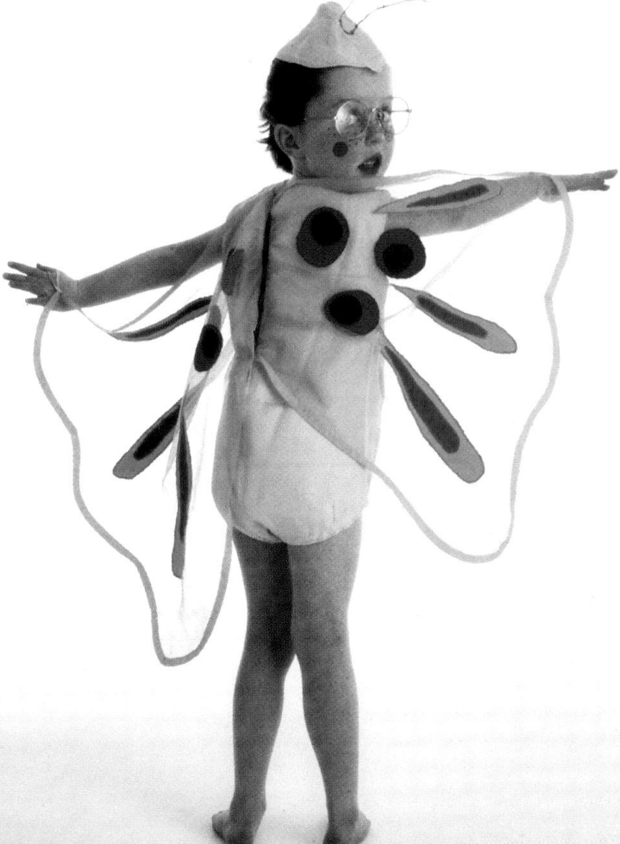

I am a robot.

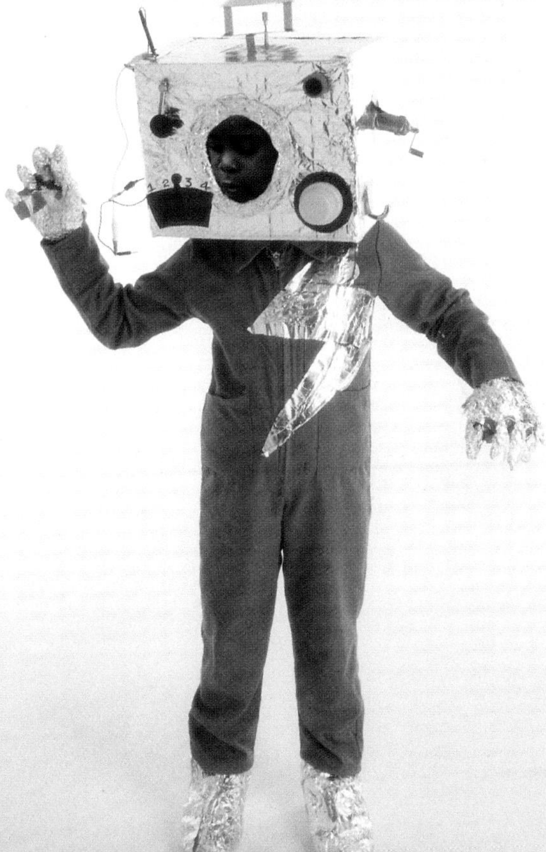
1 2 3 4

I am a dinosaur.

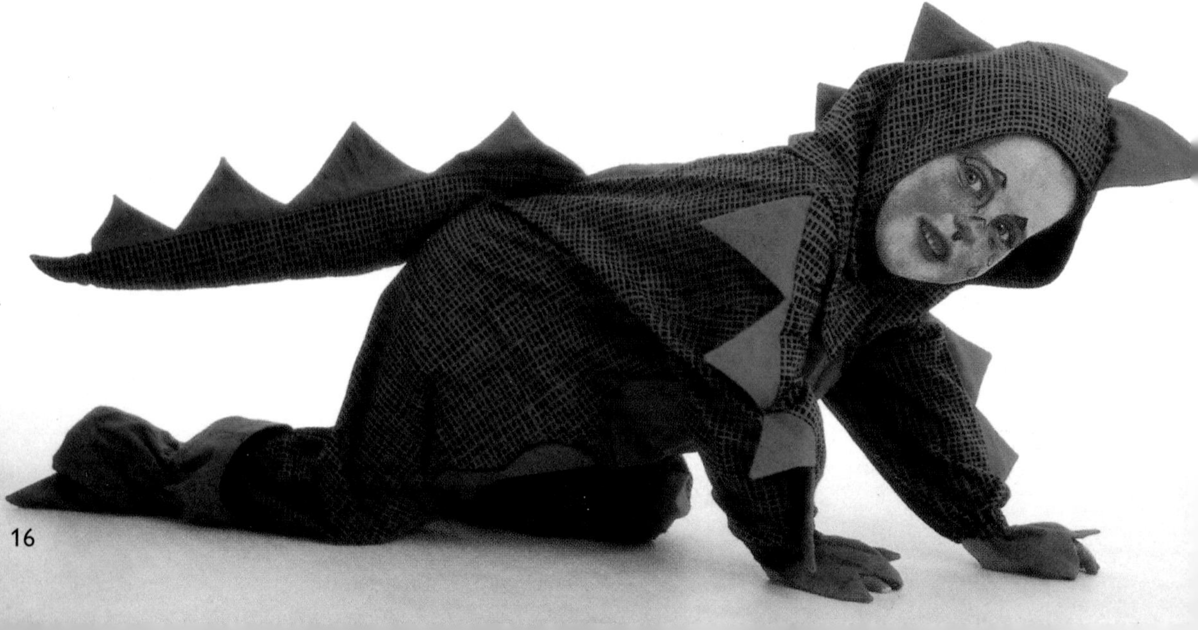